RN
HILLS

LONDON

Marlow
Cookham
Maidenhead

Sonning
ham

Windsor

Richmond

Hampton Court
Sunbury

Gravesend

NG

NORTH DOWNS

The
Thames

Rivers · of · Britain

The Thames

Grace and Favour

Wilson Stephens

Illustrated by Gabriel White

MULLER, BLOND & WHITE

The Introductory quotation is from William Morris's
Prologue to *The Wanderers*.

First published in Great Britain in 1986 by
Muller, Blond & White Limited
55 Great Ormond Street, London WC1N 3HZ.

British Library Cataloguing in Publication Data

Stephens, Wilson
    The Thames.—(Rivers of Britain)
    1. Thames, River (England)—History
    I. Title   II. Series
    942.2   DA670.T2

    ISBN 0–584–11138–X

Printed and bound in Great Britain at The Bath Press, Avon

Springhead

FATHER Thames, now protected at his seaward end by the great new barrage, could, if we wished, make London something of a modern Venice. Perhaps our descendants will so wish. Thames, for the time being, is London's un-exploited asset.

Once Thames made London the world's greatest port. Changed ways, not least the changed ways of dock workers, altered that and Thames has to be found a new purpose, or allowed to revert to an old one — that of the capital's greatest and most endur-ing recreational source. In serving as the release for London people from the tyranny of London town, Thames has achieved a spirit of his own, a reason for being, and his own characteristic *joie de vivre*.

This friendliest of rivers throughout its long history has well fulfilled all three roles. But in this present age there is — perhaps more than ever — a need for the essential Thames character to be identified, so that the prospects for the survival of its true qualities can be faced. For Thames itself is menaced by all those very factors from which it is a natural escape — the soullessness of a consumer society, hell-bent urbanisation and technology moving too fast to be controlled: factors from which all Britain seeks deliverance before, quite simply, it is too late.

Forget six counties overhung with smoke,
Forget the snorting steam and piston stroke,
Forget the spreading of the hideous town;
Think rather of the packhorse on the down . . .

Grace and Favour

THE Thames flows for pleasure. Feathery is the only word that well describes the light and luscious and ever moving pattern of the trees that line its banks. Each summer vista has a richness and vivacity belonging more to the rural France which Corot and Pissaro caught on canvas, than to our rough island weather.

Every bend opens a new vision of sweeping space and watery freshness. The river glides serenely on, a majestic progress flanked by settings which bespeak *sans souci*, even dalliance. The Thames world is an idyllic world, its idylls curiously emphasised by the occasional litter loutery, shut off from tiresome reality by those selfsame trees.

Nature has lined the banks and eyots with poplar and aspen, with crack willow and the weeping kind which trails its tendrils in the water, with alders that form caves of green light over backwaters, tall chestnuts that nod away the hours, and beds of osiers filling-in the eddies. All these are among the most frothy, responsive and bobbish of trees.

Hardly a zephyr blows so gently that it cannot awaken and enliven them all. Poplars sway as in a waltz, willows curtsey, alders toss their crowns. By happy chance the foliage of all of them is green on the upper side, but pale on the reverse, shading through grey to silver.

When the leaves dance, the ripple of movement is picked up and magnified by the alternating shades. The Thames-side view is never static, always charged with a kind of dappled energy. In that tree-lined ambit, life is to be enjoyed. To find acceptable substitutes for the groves of Arcady is seldom difficult.

The proposition that a river's nature is as much a matter of human tides as of travelling water, has a double application here. Either the river moulds the human element or, as has happened to the Thames, the human element defines the river.

Upstream of its tidal mileage, which not long ago contained the world's greatest port, England would not have been much poorer if the Thames had never existed; but it would have been much less enjoyable. Geographically insignificant, economically dispensable, historically negligible, its worth is measured by its place in human affection. The music hall image of Old Father Thames is founded on a sentiment as deep as it is universal, and the image is strengthened by the powerful mortal urge of nostalgia.

More people see the Thames in London than elsewhere. Uninspiring though its suburban and metropolitan reaches often are, they are memorable to those who come to see the capital's sights, still more so to journeymen, and women, from far away homes who have become Londoners while they seek their fortunes. That dull flood, tossing its overload of detritus between the bridges, gaining fame and even a little prestige from a charitable electorate by lapping the Houses of Parliament, expresses the landscape they have left, the England out of town.

It has arrived from the country and it is not going back, welcome proof that the roaring streets, soaring buildings, and the hustle they enclose are not the world's sum total. Long remembered small-town scenes upriver, and scarcely imagined faraway places abroad all seem nearer because the familiar old Thames is "rolling along, down to the mighty sea" — away from the known and toward the strange. The fact that the sea in question is by no means mighty, in truth no more than the fag end of the narrow seas, reflects the rosy glow of illusion.

Upriver, the Thames is thus a kind of paradise. For those too long in city pent, it is the gateway of somewhere to go to ease the pressure, to see green fields, to take a lady-love, briefly or permanently to lead the good life. So it has been since Chaucer's time, perhaps before. That search for peace was the impulsion that led medieval men of means to move out from London along the banks of Thames, to live in the freshness and sweet air of Walworth and Lambeth, and to name one small enclave Lavender Hill.

Later, when roads had improved, they extended the commuting range beyond Vauxhall to Battersea, Putney, Fulham and Hammersmith. When trains superceded coaches, the range went even wider. Staines, Maidenhead, Marlow, Mapledurham and other riverside villages grew with the influx of neo-Thames-side families. The river was magnetising man, as rivers do, all through the railway era of snorting steam and piston stroke.

Now we look on those vanished days as part of a golden age — polluted certainly, but preferable to the pollutions the Thames valley now might have — toward which we would gladly turn back the clock, in quest of remembered innocence. What has been seems better than what is. Improvements, when they come, must first grow old before they are recognised, by which time the defects they removed have faded from mind. Already we have forgotten the six counties overhung with smoke, because the smoke has been eliminated.

My working life began in Reading. The affection which I retain for that erupting conurbation does not blind me to its status as a prime example of a hideous town, nor to the evidence that it and others continue to spread. In spite of them, the fact remains that Thames and Thames-side have been rescued from defilement in other very substantial ways.

This process, so well pressed home in our own time, is still continuing. For fugitives from over-population, concrete environments, fumes of fossilised fuels, self-frustrating speed of life, depersonalisation, obligatory trivia and other characteristics of over-communalised living, the packhorse on the down is less unreal a vision than it was. It is the Thames that makes this possible.

Many rivers are born anonymous. The Thames is one of them, and it travels far before being accorded its patronymic. Its source is Seven Springs, four miles south of Cheltenham on the Gloucestershire Cotswolds. Keen eyes, even some imagination are needed to discern more than one spring, but seven is a magic number in rural lore, its repute inherited from some race long-lost among our who-knows-how-remote ancestors, so the other six must be there, somewhere.

Close research is not recommended, because their slow-seeping patch of damp is now part of the central reservation at a traffic intersection on the road to Cirencester. The outflow is named as the river Churn on the map, but not by local residents.

Englishmen, their topographical purview concentrated on what they can see and stand upon, have little interest in how other people name the outgoing versions of their village streams. In this case the Cartographer-Royal, the Prime Minister, the Archbishop of Canterbury, the President of the MCC and any other persons of prestige and influence are welcome to call this emergent rill the river Churn, if doing so gives them pleasure. But those who live there know perfectly well that it is really no more than the Rendcomb brook, and so it is hailed until the village of that name lies upstream, and the little river is well clear of North Cerney.

By the time Cirencester is reached, only a foolhardy man would deny it the courtesy name of Churn, recognising that it stands to inherit the title 'Thames' in due course. There are some, perhaps

heirs to a tradition of inter-village rivalry generations back, who still claim the name Thames Head for a winterbourne some miles further on. This all-too-modest stream is held in contempt and ridicule up-valley, because it flows only one year in three, and not always then.

Now generally accepted, the Churn flows on beside the road between Latton and Cricklade, a lively brook which passers-by are more likely to associate with tiddlers than with cargo ships in the Pool of London. Reinforced by Flagham brook, the Swill brook, and the minor river Ray, it then grows big enough to be called Thames for a mile or two. But not much farther.

Before Lechlade is reached, its name has changed to Isis, and so it remains for many more miles, until Oxford is left behind and Abingdon finds it finally and irreversibly the Thames. How came this so? One cannot tell, only guess.

Perhaps romantics of a past century, wishing to dissociate the river of their dreams from the river of commerce, and of the squalor that for so long was London, revived the ancient name Isis. Certainly Thames was a dirty word for more than a century.

But Thames he now is, in his prime all the way to Shepperton where London begins and the magic alters. And Thames he stays, though whether Father Thames precisely expresses his relationship is open to doubt. Paternity seems too positive a role for so jovial an entity; Thames is more like a jolly old uncle, always on hand and full of good cheer, but taken seriously by few.

The Good Life Downstream

ENGLAND'S eventual past flowed to and fro, without Thames playing a heroic part or proving more than a minor inconvenience. Only the ever-cautious William the Conqueror made the river a major factor in his calculations. When London's was the only bridge between Oxford and the sea, he marched all the way from Hastings to Wallingford before crossing it, then arrived at the capital from the North, via Berkhamsted. What his infantry said about the extra mileage would be interesting to know.

Later soldiers took the Thames more lightly, Cavaliers and Roundheads coming and going as if it was not there. In our own time, apart from providing most of London's water, and draining more counties than the six called Home, Thames has been short on social service, brightening the lives of its devotees instead.

No river could have a more attractive presentation. As if there had been an agreement to put the most inviting public face on Thames, the rustics down the ages chose names to mark its features which breathe tranquillity and imagery, or ring like poetry. Materially and in ideas, Thames is always evocative.

Its origin, the Churn itself, has the sound of a stoney brook. Windrush and Evenlode, the Cotswold tributaries, carry the voice of those open, peaceful hills. Others, more prosaically named, help by their character to establish the Thames conglomerate.

On the north bank, Leach and Coln from Gloucestershire, the Cherwell from high Oxfordshire, and Hertfordshire's Colne are spring-fed, sparkling streams. From the south come the Kennet; the quiet Loddon, its broadwaters skimmed by swallows as the sun goes down over ducal Stratfieldsaye; the delectable little Pang; the Wey from the pine and heather country; and the forest-born Mole from dis-

tant Sussex. These veins of southern England, reaching far and wide, link contrasting counties to the Thames.

On the river itself, men have so named favoured spots that the mere sound of them calls up their spirit, and helps legends to grow. For generations to whom foreign travel was impossible, Boulter's Lock, Cookham Dean and Maidenhead were as romantic as San Tropez and Marrakesh have since become. In days when incomes were lower and travel costly, denying Scottish salmon-fishing to all but the very rich, the stuff of anglers' dreams was woven round Penton Hook, Shiplake Hole and Bablock Hythe, where men sat in subtle battles of wits through summer heat and winter chill. More adventurous fishermen did great deeds on the aprons and mill pools, such as Bray, Odney, Hambleden and Eynsham. He who held a Thames Conservancy licence "to go upon the weirs" walked tall.

Thames banks are lined with inns where the signs have long been symptomatic of good times had by all. Seldom are they separated from the river, or from its connotations of boats and fishing and thirst. There are Anglers both Compleat and Jolly, Anchors, Leathern Bottles, Beetle and Wedges, Rings of Bells and (the higher the more frequent) Trouts — most notably at Tadpole Bridge and Lechlade.

To these haunts there came — indeed still come, though different now — all sorts and conditions of men, some with families, some most specifically without. The raffishness of Georgian Vauxhall spread upriver, infiltrating the proprieties of Ascot, a strange blending overlooked by such stately homes as Cliveden, Remenham, and even Windsor Castle.

For some, the sole objective was jellied eels and beer in appetising air; for others, the pursuit of love in the privacies of punt or skiff; or simply to be seen; for others again, the wonders of nature; or sheer lust for sunshine and fresh air. But the stabilising element, the influence that linked the years and set the tone — although often enough a tone as subtle and unobtrusive as the skill he exercises — was by Thames tradition, the fisherman.

The Thames as it was, is now on the rim of living memory. That was the Thames of Jerome K. Jerome and his friends in the boat; the Thames of those whose visits there solidified into a cult. Those were the days when fishing was a social occasion, not reduced as it is now to commuting journeys to and from the water.

Travel by train and horse-cab precluded getting there and back in a day. Where a man fished, he slept, and where he did these things, he also drank and told tall stories. The robust, convivial style which accompanied mankind's most effective care-dropper, permeated the Thames-side way of life. Relax and enjoy it; this became the motif of even the most serious anglers.

Those were also the days before social strati-fication imposed its curious code on the sport; before differentials in income group separated not only man from man, but to some extent man from fish. The combined effect is that the species of fish which a man catches has been determined since the second world war by his financial status; if he can afford salmon, he does not catch roach.

Mighty Trout and Tall Stories

THE archetypal Thames fisherman before the wars could not catch salmon, because there were none; so he caught everything else that was going, and had much fun in doing so. Part of it lay in the network of private rivalries which grew up among groups of friends based on fishing inns up and down the river.

Parties from the Stock Exchange, the law courts,

hospitals, even the mother of Parliaments would make a favoured inn their own. All the rich variety of one of the nation's finest mixed fisheries concerned them. Apart from salmon, grayling are the only British freshwater fish which cannot be found almost everywhere in the Thames's middle reaches.

Roach and dace in the open river, bream and carp in the deeps, chub lying high in the water where willows overhang, barbel in the scours around bridge piers, trout in the weir pools, perch stalking gudgeon and bleak in backwaters, patrolling pike anywhere, and always the chance of heavyweights from any of these species. When all-round fishermen were numerous, it was no wonder that they vied with each other on the Thames. The national record

21

barbel and gudgeon were caught there, and Thames roach, perch and silver bream figure in the "Where to Fish" list of notable fish.

It was still the time, not yet far gone, of the Thames professional fishermen. They rendered the same sort of service as deerstalkers in the Highlands, or the shikaris of India. Spaced out one or two to every riverside village, they lived by watching the water and trading in guidance and information for favoured clients. They knew where every good fish lay, its favourite time and place of feeding, its individual habits and, of course, the best chances of outwitting it.

Once such a fish had been marked down and studied, a telegram would go to an interested sportsman, probably in London. No doubt some engagements would be cancelled and a booking made at the local inn, anywhere from the Bells of Ouseley up to Radcot. Then a skiff would slide silently out through an early morning mist, poled, not rowed, to avoid splash; or on a darkening evening one would return through the falling shadows with its overload of satisfaction, tales of victory, and plans for celebration.

Especially coveted fish in the winter were big pike; in the summer the barbel that lie and roll like marmalade cats on shingle banks that fast water constantly washes clean; and, most prized of all, a big Thames trout, a stone or so of fighting muscle and guile. The giants are still there, but the watchers are not. The odds are against the anglers now. There is small chance that the record held by A. E. Hobbs, the Reading architect, of more than nine hundred and fifty Thames trout (he rejected as undersized anything less than five pounds) will ever be beaten.

What caused the change? Why have the professional fishermen become extinct, or nearly so? There are more reasons than just fickle fashion. The chief difference is in the modern manner, though not in the spirit, of the Thames-side human community. The effects have been diverse, but one of them has been that the former trend-setters and largesse dispensers among fishermen do not go to the Thames any more.

They play golf, sail yachts, or go north to the salmon (now reached quickly and easily by air) when they need to escape tensions which altered times have certainly not decreased. Too many other people can do too many other things on the Thames nowadays. The loss has been in atmosphere.

Days of Wine and Music

THERE are worse things than that "snorting steam and piston stroke" which was at least confined to the railway track. Instead a comparably vibrant noise has pervaded the river itself. Power boats with their bow-waves breaking on both banks set all the river rocking. In addition there are canoeists, underwater swimmers, and sailing craft in hundreds where formerly there were only dozens.

There is much, much less peace than there used to be for those watching floats or feeling the touch on ledgers.

No longer comes still evening on. The gay life lasts into darkness and long after. The subtle skills of fishing need a calm setting, and no interruptions. Because of the long Thames tradition that the river is for the pleasure of all, restrictions are few.

Likewise, the reluctance to enforce those regulations that do exist is strong; it is hardly a Thames-like thing to do to ask anybody to desist from anything, or even to modify. But this does not alter the truth; an old order has gone, anyway for the present.

The days of wine and music in the shade of the

willows just survived the Second World War, so are not forgotten yet. The memory of them indicates how sudden and how vast has been the change in manners and modes, not only on Thames-side and in Britain, but throughout the western world. While the old gramophone spilled out ragtime and the corks popped, it was the individual's wish to present himself to herself, and vice versa, in the best possible guise.

Young men who poled a punt or sculled a skiff thought it proper to wear white duck trousers, a blazer and straw boater while they did so. Those who dressed otherwise were those who could not afford such finery, not those who saw virtue for its own sake in a drab appearance, a curious concept characteristic of our own recent days.

Even those thus deprived had their standards. A suit and a bowler hat was normal when the intention was no more than to go drinking. In general, a sense of occasion and a formality not to be despised even if it became tatty were thought necessary tributes to the Thames.

Boats went past, with fringed canopies to guard from sunburn the faces of ladies already flushed with good living. Parasols were much in evidence. Exaggerated hats crowned features sometimes agreeably tipsy. Badinage flew fast. When darkness fell, coloured lights illumined landing stages, banksides and pub gardens as the long-awaited night life thrived.

The moths and the mosquitoes flocked in, flitting round the lights while human energies did not wane.

And no matter how hearty the revels, a sort of mass decorum was maintained. Victorian, Edwardian, and even inter-war days on the Thames were for people more aware of self respect than self projection.

Since then the obsessional social levelling has changed the picture. Jeans and tee-shirts, on Thames-side as elsewhere, became temporarily *de rigeur* alike for peer and pauper, and for him and her.

The healthy sound of well-drawn corks was replaced by the suspirations of beer cans and soft-drink containers. The smooth rotation of turntables gave way to wailing from transistor radio sets. Faces, however attractive, were hidden behind shaded glasses. It all seemed a little cheap and somehow sad, a case for ichabod, a departed glory.

It was also only skin deep. Although submerged in the defensive postures of the age, the old comradeship survives. The inns retain their old-time presence, and perform their old-time function as the flywheel of Thames-side life. As ever, the company that crowds into them has a characteristically London overtone, its character ranging from elegant metropolitan man to indestructible cockney.

History has moved on, the Thames has not. As it was, it still is, under the surface. As its people were, so they still are; in their essentials.

Change, Decay
and Rescue

THE time-honoured Thames-side names remain.
And with that unconquerable British reverence
for the past, so do the heirs of the Thames oldsters of
yesteryear, the sort of saloon bar wiseacres who
could answer without hesitation if asked the where
and when of the races for the punting championship
of the Thames (contests of highly polished skills
pleasantly laced with comedy which, sadly, are a rare
case of extinction) or any other question about the
river.

The long and winding Thames remains a holiday
resort, a day's lark, a slice of life, a threshold to the
sophistication of the capital. For two centuries it was
part of a Londoner's education, as Brighton had
been in Regency times. Indeed, it has seats of learn-
ing on its banks, Eton for one. But the proper con-
duct of some of life's issues are at least as well learned
at Skindles, the Shillingford Bridge, or the Rose Revived. He who keeps his poise in the mixed social
levels of Thames resorts has passed a searching test.

Meanwhile the many-sided campaign to save the
river and its littorals from seediness, atmospheric
and environmental pollution, residential over-
encroachment and out-of-place industrialisation has
been one of the triumphs of post-war Britain. Those

in charge of many interdependent efforts have worked together to win their victory.

Not only have the six counties been rescued, so has the valley's dignity, and the river's future as a zone of health and pleasure. The need now is to consolidate the winnings of the great clean-up operations which began in Coronation year, 1953.

The Thames, which for so long was both the battlefield and the losing side, faces a promising future, though some doubts remain. Not every facet will be to everybody's taste, they are too numerous and varied for that. But the outlook is much brighter, the grounds for hope much firmer, than could have been envisaged three decades ago.

Eight years of peace had not then dispersed the aftershades of war. While every other consideration had been subservient to what was necessary for the nation to survive and win, the Thames had suffered like all else. In numerous ways, some great some small, things were not what they used to be, nor what they ought to be, and the basic shortfall was in water purity.

Pollution, minor though it was when compared to that in some rivers of the industrial north, was having its inevitable effect. A river gives and takes. Its poison, if any, spreads outward, and its effects intensify with each mile nearer to the sea.

Apart from its recreational function, the Thames

is part waterpipe, part drain for nearly the whole of London and the Home Counties. It serves twelve million people in its basin of five thousand square miles between Banbury and the Hampshire downs, Swindon and Canvey Island. It fills great reservoirs, where its water is purified; it bears away the waste from homes and industries and farms along its own hundred and forty miles and several times that length of tributaries. That waste is now purified too, but was not in days gone by.

Improving the cleansing processes to meet modern requirements was an immense and complex operation more clearly witnessed by its results than by the resources and techniques employed. It was supported by other clean-ups. The electrification which took the steam and grime out of the railways, the smoke-free zones which ended urban fog, better housing and better life-styles all helped to lift the atmospheric veils that had fallen over the Thames.

The effects, negligible in the headwaters where the young Thames was always a pastoral stream, increased cumulatively in the lower reaches. Beneath cloud-trapped vapours produced by industry and overpopulation, waterborne poisons had done deadly work. Underwater banks of sludge absorbed them and became toxic reservoirs.

Waterborne life died away wherever their infections were carried. Not a water lily, not a bulrush, not a tendril of any weed existed between Putney Bridge and the sea. Any fish that tried to swim there died. Legislators eating their strawberry teas on the House of Commons terrace breathed in the gas that rose from the putrid flow, hastening indoors when the wind came off the water. To restore London's river from public scandal to public asset was a monumental task.

But it was done. The fact of its accomplishment is best demonstrated by a simple observation. For a hundred and thirty years no salmon had swum through London upriver to the once-productive spawning areas between Molesey and Cookham. Salmon and sea-trout are running the Thames again now; not many yet, but some.

More than a hundred species of sea fish are again caught in the saltwater estuary, including mackerel, mullet, whiting and haddock. Below the metropolitan reaches the waterfowl and wading birds which travel the world from season to season are again using the Thames as wintering ground. Mallard, teal, pochard, tufted duck and shelduck are counted in thousands where they had formerly become rarities.

This concentrated influx to seaward has reinforced the duck population above London, where the waning wild life of the river has been restored to what it was. The problem was not merely that of removing the smoke and steam. Sterility had to be revitalised. It has happened.

Now the varied species of Thames life, human and otherwise, those perpetual and those resurrected, must solve the problems of living together. The chief of these is overcrowding. It is fine to cruise upriver, between the green and pleasant fields, the dreaming villages, through lock after lock with their evocative traditions, to see and hear the song birds, to moor occasionally where banks of loosestrife, willow herb or flags sweeten the air.

In a day one may expect to see swans, mallard in plenty, coot, dabchick, wagtails, and swallows sipping as they fly; one may hope, not always vainly, for a sight of a great crested grebe diving and resurfacing, cat-like in its sinuous movements, in its curiosity and in keeping its distance; the jewelled brilliance of a fast-passing kingfisher; the still and patient figure of the Thames's most successful fisher, a heron; perhaps to hear the sharp little voice of an unseen reed-bunting; or the neat plop of a diving vole.

Thus pictured, an upriver voyage is a water-borne idyll, an interlude of communion with the soul of Father Thames. The reality would be an interlude of communion with much else, too. Father Thames, today, is seldom found alone.

For the Young
at Heart

WHEN, by one of his last acts before his death opened the way for the Norman invasion, Edward the Confessor granted a charter for public navigation on the Thames, he could not know in how different a kingdom his writ would eventually run. More than thirty-three thousand craft are now registered to ply on the river under the legislation which he set in motion. Forty-four weirs hold back the flow so that they can do so, forty-four locks act as hydraulic lifts to raise or lower them from one water level to another.

Up and down go public pleasure boats gaily flagged and carrying a hundred or so passengers each, passing stately by large powered cruisers, houseboats, barges, yachts, racing shells and rowing dinghies in which three may be a crowd. To be waterborne on the Thames is a way of life for many, either residentially or recreationally.

The world's third oldest yacht club was formed on the Thames at Surbiton, and still exists. The Thames-raters are racing yachts designed for the middle reaches; their immense spread of canvas demands high skill on so restricted an inland water. They also demand a fairly well-lined wallet, and most Thames water sports are less expensively based.

The Thames accent is on youth — young married couples, families, the teenage group, and others having their fun near home pending the time when they can afford to think of the coast, of rivers far away, of more specialised locations. For many, thinking is as far as they get; when the time comes, they stay on the Thames. Hence the fleets of sailing dinghies based at every Thames-side town, the eights and fours and pairs and sculls that skim the water from boat-houses up and down the banks. Rowing, that great team test and thirst-provoking sport, is as much a hallmark of the Thames as are its swans. Henley, with all its pomp and international fame, is the peak of a very large pyramid, the quintessence of long traditions.

Newer sports grow against the age-old setting. Canoes now bob and battle in the tail-races of weir pools long sacred to the famous trout. If there is a conflict of interest here it will not be the only one. The Thames has always attracted more devotees than it can keep apart. Its contrasts, however, are not always between neighbours.

Close by Staines Bridge, downstream of King John's place of confrontation with the barons at Runnymede, the London Stone marks the upper limit of the City's jurisdiction over the river. Below the Stone, its character changes.

The rowing clubs, though more famous, become fewer. There is less sailing. The surface is raked by the wakes of tugs, oil barges, timber boats and colliers – the outer ripples of the world trade that, although diminished, still comes into the Thames-

side wharfs and the Pool of London. Tidal water ends at Teddington. Viewed from upstream, the green Thames ends there, too.

But not when viewed from downstream. Suburbanisation is not the end of the Thames spirit, nor has progress obliterated that latter day pilgrims' way: the towpath. Long years have passed, nearly a century, since stalwart horses eased barges upstream on the flooding tides from Putney Bridge, where the Boat Race starts, for many a mile beyond Mortlake where it ends. But still the towpath has its traffic.

Now the only alternative to the good human foot is that most agreeable of conveyances, the bicycle. Westbound towpaths along the south bank interconnect, with only minor interruptions easily negotiable by riders of enterprise, providing an exhilarating route to the countryside without actually leaving London. There is the additional advantage that a towpath is, of necessity, flat; the ratio of freewheel to pedalling is pleasantly high.

Leaving Putney, with its slight suggestion that a cyclist without a megaphone and a rowing eight to shout at is somewhat under-dressed, the elegancies of the past succeed each other on either bank. The site of Kew's ancient palace, with Cromwell's battlefield beside Syon House across the river which inspired Milton's sonnet *When the assault was intended to the city*, the Botanical Gardens and the Old Deer Park sacred now to moneyed golfers; gracious Richmond, red and Georgian; the leafiness reviving in the wide sweep past Eel Pie Island, redolent of feasting long ago and a shrine for lovers still; Teddington and the first lock; the long sweep round to quiet Thames Ditton with deer grazing the greenery over the water; to the great and gracious palace of Hampton Court, the world's finest masterpiece in red brick.

It is not the end of the towpath, but it will do for one day's journey, for there is still the journey back. Fortunately inns are plentiful; no traveller need starve or go hungry in his peep at the world beyond metropolis. Having seen it once, he will go again, returning, I suspect, with some anxiety in his heart. For he has known heart's ease and turned his back. And what he sees when he looks at the future beyond the still refreshing appearances may not give him a corresponding pleasure.

A Labour of Love

DOWNSTREAM again, no longer is this a river with pleasure at the helm. Henceforth the father figure has a harder and more purposeful face. Here come the lighters floating free on a rising tide with their multi-ton cargoes, each steered through the bridges by one man with only his sweep to act as a rudder, brought safe to anchorage by skill alone.

This is where every curl of every current is ancestral knowledge, learned and handed down generation by generation by the watermen and lightermen whose guilds were flourishing when Agincourt was fought. They, with the fire floats, the police boats and the pleasure steamers, are the heirs to the urban dinghies that swarmed in bygone centuries and may one day swarm again.

The metropolitan river stinks no longer. In the cleaner air that now blows from it Handel's gorgeous Water Music would not come amiss. Thirty years ago we could have said only that a glory had departed. Now the prospect is of a new version of such glory returning.

The barrier at Woolwich Reach, which can cut off London from the tide or hold the river at half-tide according to need, may soon change the rivermouth entirely, and for the better. The water purity now regained opens up the concept of a great water park seaward of London, with all its possibilities for water sports and for transport. Water buses, taxi launches, goods delivery by water — all former services in central London — may yet transform the metropolitan map and by easing the traffic in the streets transform it for the better.

Not all the future view is quite as rosy, if the Thames is to be true to itself in and after AD 2000. The will to preserve the river itself is strong enough, with its pleasures and the atmosphere in which they are enjoyed, varying from exhilarating to placid. What may not be equally and adequately strong is the means of doing so.

The wish of those who love the Thames is that things should remain as they have been. But institutions and attitudes change as much as times do. It remains to be seen whether its valley's airs and graces continue to be as carefully guarded by those who now have overall responsibility for the Thames, and to whom the Thames is by present definition a public utility rather than a public amenity. Already nomenclature foreshadows a change in emphasis. There are hopes on many sides that the shadows will prove to have no substance.

The Thames is what it is because of its former governing body, the Thames Conservancy. That name alone spoke volumes. Its members represented popular tradition as well as general competence. Residential qualification stood high in their requirements.

Hence the Conservancy consisted of people indoctrinated in the Thames-side outlook; the name expressed what they were called upon to do. Know-

ledge of the river, belief in the river, understanding of the river's full part in the life of its region, and a share in the pleasures of others who loved the river, all impelled them in the discharge of their function.

This was to conserve the river in the fullest sense. It did not stop at exploiting the river in the fulfilment of the basic public requirements of water supply and drainage.

There may or may not be much in a name. One hopes there is not, in this case. Nevertheless there is less overt recognition of the role's full breadth in the designation of the Conservancy's successor body, the Thames Water Authority.

The overtones of the word Authority may prove to be undeserved on the Thames. Nevertheless there are many who are already suspicious of the frequency with which the terms "business" and "businesslike" have occurred in the Authority's pronouncements, and of the apparent weight given to them.

In the administrative newspeak of our time, "business" often implies actions governed by short term calculations and narrow-focus vision. The hazard is that, those seeing overmuch merit in a "business" attitude (which is not necessarily an efficient one in the wider sense) may regard any environment as satisfactory which is cost-effective. Thames people, looking for something more imaginative and more intelligent, were already anxious as the bodeful year of 1984 slid into the past.

The clean-up, with its huge success, had achieved the Authority's hydrological requirements. The next need has been to safeguard less material and more vulnerable factors — the Thames's public face and its non-aqueous utilities. Historically, these had never been neglected.

Realistically, the problems they pose are greater and more numerous, not less, as a result of that clean-up. The first of the problems, and the origin of many others, is pressure of numbers.

Extra leisure, some enforced by unemployment, a cleaner prospect, and growing affluence must have identical effects on the Thames. They give more people the time or the money or the wish to visit the river. The influx of car-towed sail craft grows; every launching place from Lechlade downstream sends more boats out on to the water. Cabin cruisers and canoes are now to be added to the traditional wind-blown and muscle-propelled craft.

There is less and less water for each individual keel. The fishermen, the naturalists, the scenery seekers, and the idlers also come, and a great divide grows between the makers of noise and disturbance, and the lovers of peace and quiet. By its nature, a river favours the latter.

Engines afloat, outboard and otherwise, now earn the opprobrium previously aroused by snorting steam in the land background. Fishermen hope for an unchurned water surface; naturalists for a silence

in which to hear birdsong, solitude in which to study wild flowers, an absence of the sort of surprise which an emerging sub-aqua swimmer inflicts on an observer of dragon flies; others look for the seemliness which makes the Thames a pleasant place. These are issues which have already arisen. The question is: who is to resolve them and others like them henceforth, and how?

It is obvious that they can be reconciled only by codes of discipline in river recreation preventing such interests encroaching on others. Preferably it will be self-discipline, but humanity is fallible and sometimes enforcement will be needed. It is imperative that it should not look like enforcement.

Too obtrusive a corps of wardens would negate the friendly Thames spirit as surely as inaction may destroy it. The tone could be well taken from the experience of the Thames Navigation inspectors, their practised techniques in friendly persuasion backed by powers to arrest and prosecute, used as seldom as possible.

No less important is the appearance of the lush and civilised Thames. Nature cannot provide all the beauty where so much else is man-made. The ultimate truth which has made the Thames what it is, and which alone can keep Thames sweet for ever, is the human touch.

In a utilitarian era, the idea of dedication must be kept alive or Thames, so long the silver lining to the London cloud, will lose its lustre. Present evidence is that the Thames Water Authority, itself the heir to long and proud traditions in the provision of man-

kind's most basic necessity, is aware of its grace and favour element as well. The doubt concerns the continued place of that element in the priorities.

Success in maintaining it will be a matter of art, not science. Beauty and the zest for living cannot be commanded, created, or directed as can water, or money. It is a matter of upholding standards in countless ways which may seem small when viewed against central commitments, but are not trivial.

That fish should swim in the Thames; that men, women and children should peacefully enjoy its healthy pleasures; that those who look around them should find a scene which gives inspiration and rest of heart are none of them conditions essential to human survival. But they are essential to the proper fullness of the human spirit.

They can be destroyed by management decision, but cannot be re-created by other management decisions. They can be kept in being only by effort applied to local details by innumerable people innumerable times. This demands wide response to what has been demonstrated so amply for centuries, love of the river.

The celebrated weirkeepers' gardens beside the locks, which hit the headlines every year, were never a mere conceit. Pride of place has ensured that those who live on the banks of Thames, and those who visit them, see flowers at their feet. Pride of place requires that there should be something to be proud of.

The simplicities of the days when the packhorse on the down bore the wealth of England in fleeces on his back, or the pedlars' stock-in-trade, will not return to the world as it now is. But the Thames itself is a simplicity, and in that sense a release. Its destiny can keep it so, but only if we let it.

Illustrations

THE THAMES

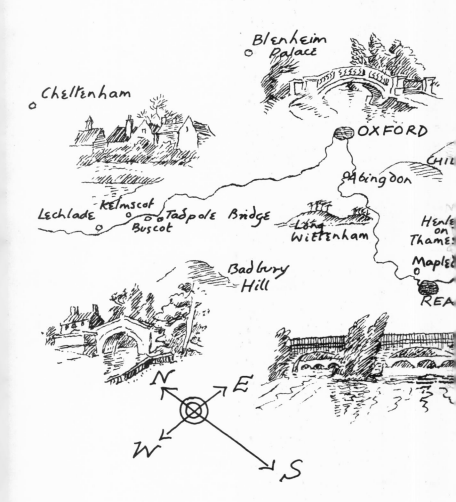

Blenheim Palace

Cheltenham

OXFORD

CHIL

Abingdon

Lechlade Kelmscot Tadpole Bridge
Buscot

Long Wittenham

Henle on Thames

Mapls

Badbury Hill

REA

N E
W S